CONTENTS

A GHOSTLY WORLD

Since ancient times, people have believed in the afterlife (life after death) and ghosts. Ancient Egyptians believed that you would need your body in the next life, so they mummified the bodies of the dead to preserve them. Romans believed that the spirits of their ancestors, called larvae, returned as ghosts to haunt the living.

CELEBRATIONS
Halloween, on 31st October, was traditionally the night ghosts walked the Earth. Bonfires were lit to summon the spirits and please them by keeping them warm. On the Day of the Dead, in Mexico, (2nd November) people remember and celebrate those who have died.

Today, Halloween is celebrated with homemade jack-o'-lanterns (above) and children playing 'Trick or treat?'

A skeleton dressed in white (above) decorates the front of a shop during the Mexican Day of the Dead.

GRAPHIC MYSTERIES

GHOSTS AND POLTERGEISTS

STORIES OF THE SUPERNATURAL

by David West

illustrated by Terry Riley

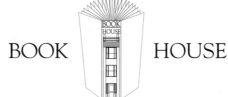

BOOK HOUSE

Designed and produced by
David West 👥 Children's Books
7 Princeton Court
55 Felsham Road
London SW15 1AZ

Editor: Dominique Crowley

Photo credits:
Page 4 (bottom left), Max Azison; page 4 (bottom right), Teresa Hurst; page 5 (top right), Peter Guess, Dreamstime.com; page 6, Katherine Garrenson; page 7, Image provided by Dreamstime.com; page 44-45, Hermann Danzmayr.

First published in 2006 by **Book House,**
an imprint of **The Salariya Book Company Ltd**
25 Marlborough Place, Brighton BN1 1UB

Please visit the Salariya Book Company at:
www.salariya.com

HB ISBN 1 905087 79 9
PB ISBN 1 905087 80 2

Visit our website at **www.book-house.co.uk**
for free electronic versions of:
You Wouldn't Want to Be an Egyptian Mummy!
You Wouldn't Want to Be a Roman Gladiator!
Avoid joining Shackleton's Polar Expedition!

A catalogue record for this book is available from the British Library.

Printed on paper from sustainable forests.

Manufactured in China.

FAVOURITE HAUNTS

Many people believe that graveyards are the most likely place to see a ghost. According to folklore however, ghosts haunt the places where they died. When a new graveyard was built in the Dark Ages, pagans sacrificed victims so that their spirits would become the new graveyard's guardians. People have often reported seeing strange lights in graveyards, believing them to be ghosts. Today, scientists think they are probably luminous gases rising from the rotting corpses.

Haunted houses are far more common places to come across ghosts, especially if a person has been murdered or buried in the house. Both 112 Ocean Avenue, Amityville, New York (see page 22), and Borley Rectory, Essex, are reportedly the most haunted houses in the world.

Graveyards are actually unlikely haunts for ghosts.

Borley Rectory, in Essex, (below) was the scene of ghostly hauntings by a nun from 1927 until it burnt down in 1939. On inspection, bones of a young woman were found under the cellar floor.

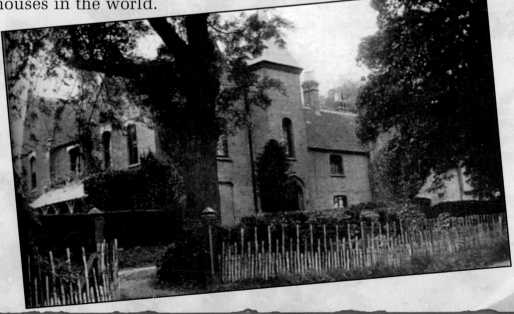

WHAT IS A GHOST?

The traditional representation of a ghost as a person under a sheet has become more sophisticated as more and more ghost films hit the silver screen and computer-generated special effects improve.

GRAPHIC MYSTERIES
GHOSTS AND POLTERGEISTS

FROM SHAKESPEARE TO HOLLYWOOD
Ghosts have been portrayed in literature from the days of the ancient Greeks. The Greek poet Homer, c. 750 B.C., described the ghost of Hector in his epic poem the *Iliad*. Early Chinese literature and Roman writings also describe ghosts. Most famously of all, William Shakespeare (1564–1616) wrote plays with ghostly goings-on such as *Hamlet* and *Macbeth*. In *A Christmas Carol* (1843), by Charles Dickens, a miser called Scrooge is visited by three ghosts. Today, cinema has kept the image of ghosts firmly in our minds with classic films such as *Poltergeist* (1982), *Ghostbusters* (1984), *Ghost* (1989) and the remake of *The Amityville Horror* (2005). See page 22 onwards for the events on which this last film is based.

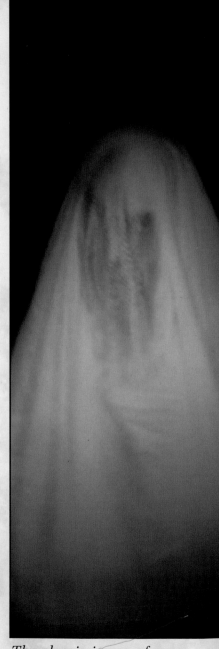

The classic image of a ghost is of a person draped in a white sheet.

TYPES OF GHOSTS

Ghosts or spirits can appear in different forms and have a definite purpose, according to some believers. They might visit people to give warnings, take revenge on those who have hurt them, or request that their bodies be buried properly so their spirits can rest in peace. A few of the better-known spirits from around the world are described in the panel (right).

GETTING IN TOUCH

People called mediums claim to be able to contact the dead. One way of doing this is to gather a group of people round a table. They all hold hands. The medium calls up the spirit of the dead person and acts as an intermediary between the spirit and its living relatives. This is called a séance. It has been claimed that sometimes mediums have helped police to catch murderers.

GHOSTLY FORMS

Banshee – an Irish ghost in the form of a screaming woman. It forewarns a person of his or her time of death.

Duppy – an evil Jamaican spirit said to live in the buttress roots of silk cotton trees.

Ghoul – an Arabian demon that lives in the desert. It is said to suck the blood of humans.

Jinnie – a Middle Eastern spirit made of smokeless fire. A jinnie can be controlled with magic by binding it to an object, such as a lamp, as in the story of Aladdin.

Poltergeist – an invisible ghost that is violent, noisy, and can even cause fires. It is believed to be active around teenagers who are troubled.

Virika – a small, red, evil spirit from India. A virika will roam about at night making strange gibbering noises.

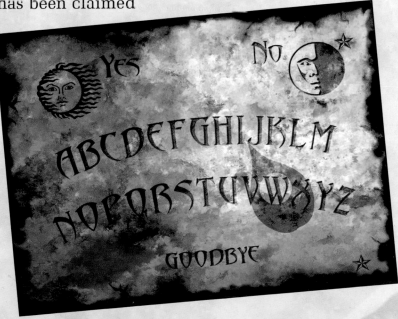

Ouija boards are used to 'talk' with the dead. A number of people put their fingers on a small glass, which the spirit then moves to answer questions by spelling out words.

LORD DUFFERIN AND THE GHOSTLY APPARITION

1880, TULLEMORE, COUNTY WEXFORD, IRELAND. LORD DUFFERIN IS STAYING AT THE HOUSE OF A FRIEND.

THE NEXT MORNING, LORD DUFFERIN TELLS HIS HOST WHAT HAPPENED THE PREVIOUS NIGHT.

...HE WAS THE UGLIEST MAN I HAVE EVER SET EYES ON. THEN, UPON MY WORD, THE FELLOW VANISHED IN FRONT OF MY OWN EYES.

HOW VERY ODD. THERE IS NO SUCH PERSON HERE-ABOUTS. AND I DO ASSURE YOU, MY LORD, WE HAVE NEVER SEEN A GHOST IN THESE PARTS.

A FEW YEARS LATER, AT THE GRAND HOTEL, PARIS, LORD DUFFERIN IS ATTENDING A DIPLOMATIC FUNCTION.

THIS WAY, MY LORD. WE WILL NEED TO TAKE THE LIFT.

SHHCLANG

THE LIFT OPERATOR. HE'S THE SAME MAN I SAW CARRYING THE COFFIN IN TULLEMORE.

KERRRACK

THE LIFT PLUMMETS TO THE GROUND KILLING ALL THE OCCUPANTS.

I SAY!

AAAARRRGH!

OH, HEAVENS!

THE ACCIDENT WAS INVESTIGATED, BUT NOBODY EVER FOUND OUT WHO THE STRANGE LIFT OPERATOR WAS. **THE END**

THE MACOMB POLTERGEIST

7 AUGUST, 1948, WILLEY'S FARM, MACOMB, ILLINOIS, USA.

HEY, CAN ANYONE SMELL BURNING?

DAD, WHY CAN'T I STAY WITH MUM IN BLOOMINGTON?

MAYBE IT'S THE STOVE.

LISTEN WANET, WE'VE BEEN THROUGH THIS BEFORE...

WANET, AGE 13, AND HER BROTHER, ARTHUR JUNIOR, AGE 8, LIVE WITH THEIR FATHER ARTHUR McNEIL, AFTER THEIR PARENTS' DIVORCE. THEY ARE ALL STAYING WITH THEIR RELATIVES, MR. AND MRS. CHARLES WILLEY.

BUT IT'S SO UNFAIR!

HEAVEN HELP US! THE WOOD BOX IS ON FIRE!

11 AUGUST. BROWN SPOTS APPEAR ON THE WALLPAPER AND BURST INTO FLAME.

12 AUGUST. NEIGHBOURS HELP THE FAMILY TO TEAR DOWN THE WALLPAPER.

SHOOT! LOOK AT THAT! BROWN MARKS ARE APPEARING IN THE PLASTER!

HEY, WALTER! CAN YOU GET SOME MORE WATER?

SURE THING!

AW, HECK! WOULD YA LOOK AT THAT? UGH! IT WAS A LACE CURTAIN FIVE MINUTES AGO.

THE MACOMB FIRE CHIEF, FRED WILSON, WHO SUGGESTED STRIPPING THE WALLPAPER, IS BAFFLED. WITH HIM IS THE STATE FIRE MARSHAL, JOHN BURGARD.

LOOK! THEY'RE APPEARING ON THE CEILING!

I'VE NEVER SEEN ANYTHING LIKE THIS BEFORE.

13 AUGUST. THE WILLEY'S HOME BURNS DOWN COMPLETELY.

MCNEIL MOVES HIS CHILDREN INTO THE WILLEY'S GARAGE. CHARLES WILLEY SETS UP A TENT FOR HIS FAMILY TO LIVE IN TEMPORARILY.

WE'RE GONNA LIVE IN A GARAGE NOW? YOU GOTTA BE KIDDING, DAD!

OH MY GOODNESS! NOW THE BARN'S ON FIRE!

THE NEXT DAY, THE DAIRY, WHICH WAS BEING USED AS A DINING ROOM, GOES UP IN FLAMES.

TWO DAYS LATER...

LOOK OUT! THERE'S ANOTHER FIRE!

WE HEARD ABOUT YOUR TROUBLES. THESE ARE THE LATEST IN FIRE EXTINGUISHERS...

FIRE! FIRE!

THAT AFTERNOON, THE SECOND BARN BURNS DOWN. THE HEAT IS TOO INTENSE EVEN FOR THE NEW FIRE EXTINGUISHERS.

20

WHAT'S GOING ON, MR. SCOTT?

WE'VE FOUND THE CULPRIT. WANET MCNEIL HAS ADMITTED TO STARTING THE FIRES WITH A BOX OF MATCHES.

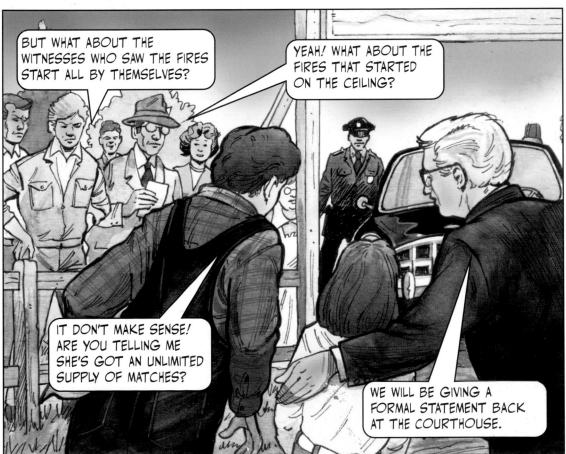

BUT WHAT ABOUT THE WITNESSES WHO SAW THE FIRES START ALL BY THEMSELVES?

YEAH! WHAT ABOUT THE FIRES THAT STARTED ON THE CEILING?

IT DON'T MAKE SENSE! ARE YOU TELLING ME SHE'S GOT AN UNLIMITED SUPPLY OF MATCHES?

WE WILL BE GIVING A FORMAL STATEMENT BACK AT THE COURTHOUSE.

ALTHOUGH THE STORY DIED DOWN QUICKLY, MOST PEOPLE WERE NOT CONVINCED BY WANET'S CONFESSION. MANY PARANORMAL INVESTIGATORS THINK THE FIRES AT THE WILLEY'S FARM WERE THE WORK OF A POLTERGEIST.   THE END

THE HAUNTED HOUSE AT AMITYVILLE

FEBRUARY 1976. A REPORTER FROM NEW YORK'S LOCAL TELEVISION STATION, WNEW, IS BROADCASTING LIVE...

WE ARE OUTSIDE 112 OCEAN AVENUE, AMITYVILLE, LONG ISLAND, WHERE A SÉANCE IS BEING HELD BY ED AND LORRAINE WARREN, TWO OF AMERICA'S MOST FAMOUS DEMONOLOGISTS.

THEY ARE INVESTIGATING CLAIMS BY THE HOMEOWNERS THAT THE HOUSE IS HAUNTED. GEORGE AND KATHY LUTZ, AND THEIR THREE CHILDREN, SAY THEY FLED FOR THEIR LIVES AFTER SPENDING ONLY 28 DAYS HERE.

SOME OF YOU MAY REMEMBER THAT THIS SAME HOUSE WAS RECENTLY THE SCENE OF A GRISLY MURDER.

ONLY 14 MONTHS AGO, RONALD DEFEO JUNIOR MURDERED HIS ENTIRE FAMILY WITH A HIGH-POWERED RIFLE AS THEY SLEPT.

DEFEO CLAIMED THAT, AT THE TIME OF THE SHOOTING, HE HEARD VOICES URGING HIM TO DO IT.

I CAN TELL YOU THAT EARLIER TODAY, I WALKED AROUND THE HOUSE WITH THE WARRENS, AND I HOPE THAT IS AS CLOSE TO HELL AS I EVER G... WAIT! IT LOOKS LIKE THERE'S BEEN A DEVELOPMENT...

PUT HER DOWN HERE.

THAT PLACE IS PURE EVIL. I'LL NEVER GO BACK IN THERE!

WHAT HAPPENED?

LORRAINE CONTACTED THE EVIL SPIRITS. IT WAS TERRIFYING. ONE OF THE INVESTIGATORS FAINTED FROM FRIGHT!

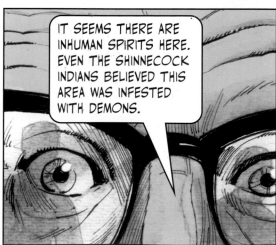

IT SEEMS THERE ARE INHUMAN SPIRITS HERE. EVEN THE SHINNECOCK INDIANS BELIEVED THIS AREA WAS INFESTED WITH DEMONS.

AS YOU CAN SEE FROM THIS TAPE, THE TOP PSYCHIC INVESTIGATORS ARE SAYING THE HOUSE IS DEFINITELY HAUNTED.

...THIS AREA WAS INFESTED WITH DEMONS...

OH, I BELIEVE YOU. WELL, IF I'M GOING TO WRITE YOUR STORY, YOU'D BETTER TELL ME EXACTLY WHAT HAPPENED.

OK. BUT SO MUCH HAPPENED IN SUCH A SHORT TIME, I'M NOT SURE IF I'LL GET EVERYTHING IN THE RIGHT ORDER.

THAT'S ALL RIGHT. JUST GIVE ME THE BARE BONES TO BEGIN WITH. WE'LL FLESH OUT THE DETAILS LATER.

"WE BOUGHT THE HOUSE AND MOVED IN ON 18TH DECEMBER, 1975. WE KNEW ABOUT THE MURDERS, BUT IT DIDN'T BOTHER US. WE DIDN'T BELIEVE IN GHOSTS BACK THEN."

COME ON, YOU THREE. LET'S GET UNPACKED.

"I HAD INVITED A PRIEST TO BLESS THE HOUSE."

HELLO FATHER MANCUSO.

HELLO, HELLO. WHAT A LOVELY HOUSE. YOU CARRY ON UNPACKING. I'LL START AT THE TOP AND MEET YOU DOWNSTAIRS.

IN THE NAME OF THE FATHER...

...THE SON AND THE HOLY SPIRIT...

GET OUTA

...WHAT THE...?

26

IS EVERYTHING ALL RIGHT FATHER?

YES, YES. EVERYTHING IS FINE. JUST ONE SMALL THING... I WOULDN'T USE THE MIDDLE ROOM UPSTAIRS AS A BEDROOM.

?!

"AS SOON AS WE MOVED IN, STRANGE AND SPOOKY THINGS STARTED HAPPENING."

WHA_?!

TARTARADATATTADUMDA

WHAT IS IT?

IT SOUNDS LIKE A MARCHING BAND IS PARADING AROUND DOWNSTAIRS!

TARTARADATATTADUMDA

A BAND IN THE HOUSE? GEORGE, IT DOESN'T MAKE SENSE.

RADATATTADUMDA

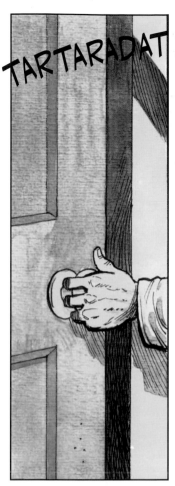

TARTARADAT

HUH? ALL THE FURNITURE HAS BEEN MOVED.

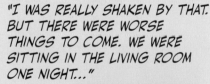

"I WAS REALLY SHAKEN BY THAT. BUT THERE WERE WORSE THINGS TO COME. WE WERE SITTING IN THE LIVING ROOM ONE NIGHT..."

TRRRRRRR

WHAT ON EARTH?

WH...WHERE DID IT GO?

IT'S DISAPPEARED. BUT LOOK! THERE'S A MARK WHERE IT WAS.

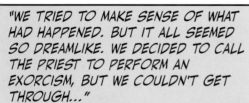

"WE TRIED TO MAKE SENSE OF WHAT HAD HAPPENED. BUT IT ALL SEEMED SO DREAMLIKE. WE DECIDED TO CALL THE PRIEST TO PERFORM AN EXORCISM, BUT WE COULDN'T GET THROUGH..."

EVERY TIME I RING HIM, THERE'S SOME WEIRD INTERFERENCE ON THE LINE.

HMMMMMMMMMMMMMM

DON'T WORRY. THINGS SEEM TO HAVE SETTLED DOWN NOW. WHAT'S THAT BUZZING NOISE? HAVE YOU LEFT THE PHONE OFF THE HOOK?

IT SEEMS TO BE COMING FROM UPSTAIRS.

"WHEN I WENT BACK OUTSIDE, THERE WERE TRACKS IN THE SNOW THAT HAD BEEN MADE BY CLOVEN HOOVES!"

"THEN THERE WAS THE TIME I WAS ALONE IN THE LIVING ROOM ONE NIGHT, SITTING IN A CHAIR NEXT TO OUR STATUE OF A LION..."

"THERE WERE ALSO STRANGE, SICKLY SMELLS WAFTING THROUGH THE HOUSE. THEN KATHY STARTED GETTING TOUCHED BY... WELL, YOU TELL HIM, KATHY."

"IT WAS VERY CREEPY. I WOULD BE DOING SOME HOUSEWORK, WHEN SUDDENLY I WOULD FEEL A STRANGE PRESENCE BEHIND ME...

WHA...

...INVISIBLE HANDS WOULD GRAB ME.

AAAAAHHHH!

SOMETIMES, I WOULD END UP WITH RED MARKS. ONE NIGHT, IT FELT AS IF I WAS BEING LIFTED UP! IT WAS MORE HORRIFYING FOR GEORGE THAN FOR ME."

YEAH! I WOKE UP TO SEE HER AND...

"ONE NIGHT, WE HEARD A NOISE COMING FROM A WARDROBE."

TAP CLUNK

THERE'S SOMETHING MOVING IN THERE! I HAVE TO FIND OUT WHAT IT IS!

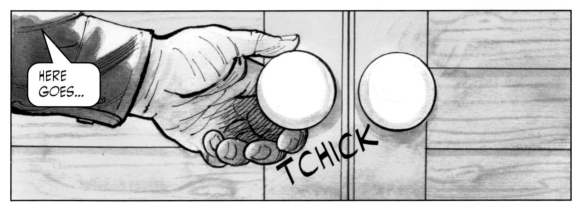

HERE GOES...

TCHICK

WHOOOSH

CLICK

OH! THIS PLACE IS PURE EVIL!!

"I THINK THAT NIGHT DID IT FOR US. WE REALISED WE COULDN'T STAY THERE ANY LONGER."

GRAB THE KIDS – WE'RE GETTING OUT OF HERE!

SCREEECH

WHAT THE...?

"WE LEFT THAT NIGHT WITHOUT TAKING ANY OF OUR STUFF, AND WE HAVE NO INTENTION OF EVER GOING BACK AGAIN."

THE END

FACT OR FICTION?

GRAPHIC MYSTERIES • GHOSTS AND POLTERGEISTS

Do ghosts really exist? Are they the returning spirits of the dead? Or are they just a trick of the light, projected by people's vivid imaginations?

THE CASE FOR

Most cultures and religions believe in life after death. Therefore, a connection between the two worlds is only a small leap of faith. Very few people have seen ghosts, and we only have their word for it as proof. Ghost hunter Andrew Green claims that you will never see a ghost if you look for it. However, some pictures have been taken of what appear to be ghostly figures. Even experts agree these are not fakes.

On 19th September, 1936, Captain Provand and Indre Shira were taking photographs for a magazine at Raynham Hall, Norfolk. Shira saw something gliding down the stairs while Provand was focusing the camera. Shira fired the flash, and the resulting photograph is shown here (left). Raynham Hall was said to be haunted by a ghost called the Brown Lady!

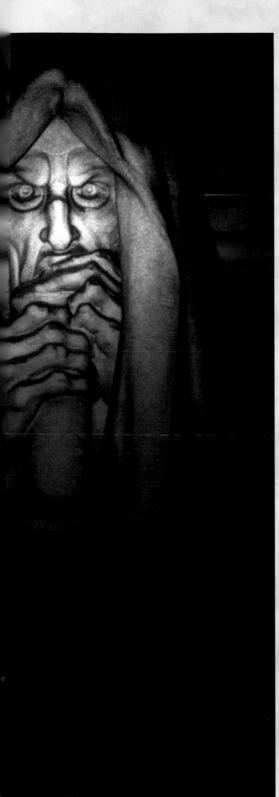

Scary otherworldly visions, like this statue in a Gothic church, continue to encourage our belief in ghosts and demons who cross over from the 'other side'.

THE CASE AGAINST

In many cases, the events of a haunting or ghost sighting have been exaggerated and distorted. The truth of these reports is often quite mundane. In 1869, photographer William Mumner was tried for selling photographs that he claimed included ghosts or spirits. In a hearing that attracted national interest, his photographs were thought to be created by darkroom techniques. All photographs of ghosts are open to charges of fraud, since the very nature of the developing process can allow for trickery, especially in today's world of computer-generated imagery.

Tricking audiences with ghostly visions at theatres in the Victorian era was easily done with the use of mirrors and glass.

GLOSSARY

afterlife The world that a person's spirit lives in after he or she has died.

apparition Appearance of a ghost or other spiritual being.

buttress roots Roots that buckle up and are seen above the soil.

cloven When the foot of an animal is divided into two parts, such as a pig's hoof.

demonologist Someone who studies demons or evil spirits.

diplomat Somebody employed by the government to represent their own country in another country.

diplomatic function A social event involving diplomats from different countries.

epic A very long poem that tells a story of adventure and often features war or romance.

exorcism The banishment of evil spirits from inside a living body or a building.

grisly Frightening and very horrible.

infest To swarm and spread over something; often refers to large groups of insects.

interference A blockage that prevents sound from being transferred. It is caused by two waves, such as sound waves, meeting each other.

intermediary A person who carries messages between two people.

Lord A male who has power and authority over others, which has been passed down to him from a deceased, older family member.

ouija board A board covered with signs and letters of the alphabet used to send questions to, and receive answers from spirits.

paranormal Something that cannot be explained.

poltergeist A ghost who is thought to create strange, loud noises.

psychic A person believed to have powers that cannot be easily explained, such as the ability to read minds.

séance A meeting in which a medium calls on spirits of the dead and passes messages between the dead and the living.

Shinnecock Indians A tribe of Native Americans who have lived for a very long time in eastern Long Island, New York, USA.

underwriter Someone who is paid small amounts of money to insure a valuable object, such as a house. If the object is damaged or stolen, the underwriter pays a large amount of money to replace or repair it.

Victorian theatre A type of dramatic performance that was popular in England during the reign of Queen Victoria. Ghosts were a popular subject of plays that were produced during this time.

FOR MORE INFORMATION

FOR FURTHER READING
If you liked this book, you might also want to try:

Bigfoot and Other Strange Beasts
by Rob Shone, Book House 2006

The Bermuda Triangle
by David West, Book House 2006

The Ghost That Haunted Itself: The Story of the McKenzie Poltergeist.
by Jan-Andrew Henderson, Mainstream Publishing 2001

Poltergeists?
by Anna Claybourne, Usbourne 1998

The Best Ghost Stories Ever.
by C Krovatin, Scholastic 2004.

Ghosts and Poltergeists, Fact or Fiction?
by T O'Neill, Greenhaven Press 2002.

INDEX

Websites

Due to the changing nature of Internet links, the Salariya Book Company has developed an online list of websites related to the subject of this book. This site is updated regularly.
Please use this link to access the list:
http://www.book-house.co.uk/grmy/ghosts